D1236691

Poems for Camilla

POEMS FOR CAMILLA

Poems by
Rachel Hadas

Measure Press
Evansville, Indiana

The text of this book is composed in Baskerville.
Composition by R.G.
Manufacturing by Ingram.

Hadas, Rachel
   Poems for Camilla / by Rachel Hadas — 1st ed.

   ISBN-13: 978-1-939574-25-1
   ISBN-10: 1-939574-25-0
   Library of Congress Control Number: 2018946867

Measure Press
526 S. Lincoln Park Dr.
Evansville, IN 47714
http://www.measurepress.com/measure/

Acknowledgments

The author would like to thank the following journals in which poems previously appeared, sometimes in slightly different form.

Classical Outlook: "The Cause" and "In Vain"
Hudson Review: "Looking On"
Plume: "Camilla"
Scoundreltime: "The Mothers on the Wall"
Think: "The Long View," "Iron Chambers," and "Stride for Stride"

* Halfway Down the Hall

For Camilla Williams
born January 17, 2017

CONTENTS

Camilla   1
The Sense of the Meeting   3
Anxiety Attack   5
Filing System   6
Stride for Stride   8
The Mothers on the Wall   9
A Female Cry   10
The Cause   11
Hope: The Secret   12
The Source of Thoughts   14
In Vain   15
Carrying the Future   17
Rejoicing in the Image   19
Ignorance   20
Grief and Solace   22
The Herbalist   24
Looking On   26
The Long View   28
Their Own Particular Day   29
And You, Catiline   30
No Way Out   32
Iron Chambers   35
Placid and Harmless   36
Iron Sleep   38
Special Effects   39
Eagle and Serpent   41
Painted Full of Tongues   43
Weaponized   45
Poetry Out Loud   46
Above and Below   48

Camilla

penitusque in viscera lapsum
serpentis furiale malum totamque pererrat
— *Aeneid* VII. 374-5

Our newborn granddaughter is named Camilla
from *Aeneid* VII's warrior maiden,
the speedy runner, skimming over wheat,
scouring the ocean, keeping her feet dry.
So there I was revisiting Camilla.
And not content with the fifteen luminous lines
evoking her, I started turning pages
backwards, and, stumbling over rage and terror,
slowed down. The appearance of the Fury
Allecto, summoned out of hell by Juno
and morphed into a serpent — maybe several —
stopped me. No more skimming
over images of devastation.
The venom oozed in, and the sickness started
To storm her senses, wrap her bones in fire —
she being Amata, Queen of Latium,
whose venerable husband, King Latinus,
is hoping for alliance with Aeneas.
But no. The snakes that slide into Amata's heart,
hang from her earrings, wreathe her throat, infuse
their venom through her body and her mind,
then flow into the women of the city
and thence they strike the sleeping hero Turnus.
Night terrors. Panic. Rage.

I read this with the pleasure,
and also with the dread, of recognition —

avid, reluctant. It was so familiar.
Haven't we all experienced this year
that rage, insidious, insatiable,
infusing crowds? Once poisonous fires are lit,
they are not easily put out. The gates
of war once open, who is strong enough
to shut them? Who has the authority?
Amata, Virgil tells us, spun — was driven —
wildly all through the city like a top
which boys in empty courtyards, *vacua atria*
(an image which evokes De Chirico's
desolate cityscapes) — which these gangs of boys
stare at in wonder. Yet they've set it going.
Does staring signify
entertainment or approval? Or
are we all simply mesmerized by motion,
by speed without direction,
out of control? We gaze and do not know
or worse perhaps do know where this is going.
The Trojan refugees, the civil war,
the dignified old king, the raving matron
stained and soaked with venom hot from hell
which once released cannot be washed away —

It was time to shut the book awhile
and think about this new
beginning, new Camilla. Curled-up morsel,
you will uncurl those legs and start to stretch
and then to crawl and then stand up and walk.
And then, Camilla, you will start to run.

The Sense of the Meeting

*It is true that the vehicle must be logically different from the
tenor, but it is also true that the basic effect depends on seeing
the similarities between two things that at first appear to be
different.*

— Norman Friedman,
Princeton Encyclopedia of Poetry and Poetics

The tenor, the idea: human discord.
A god calms stormy waters — waters stirred
to turbulence by other gods, themselves
obedient to a higher order of indignation,
also divine, that masters and controls,
choreographs the unruly seas.
So all those crashing breakers signify
nothing more than a meeting,
a faculty or committee meeting
where speakers talk and others disagree
and someone, losing patience, calls for order.

Or do we have it backwards?
The citizen whose grave authority
subdues an agitated mob which then
grows mild and calm as an unruffled sea
is really just a vehicle, a means
of heightening by this apt comparison
the tenor, the true focus, the real theme,
which in this reading is disharmony
in heaven, not on earth —
divine disputes grown rancorous and violent,
played out among the elements. Of these

our petty human quarrels
are a pallid miniature rendition.

Tenor, vehicle:
whichever way we parse it,
in any gathering disagreements rumble,
subterranean currents, the portentous
rustling of leaves before a coming storm.
All these natural tropes do correspond
to mortal passions. Boulders, rushing rivers,
tall waves, the tooth-like chattering of those leaves:
human emotions mime, reflect, enact
the flow and noise of water and of wind.

Vehicle and tenor. Which is which?
When Virgil writes of colloquies
where human doubt and discord,
crescendoing toward anger,
throb, a secret vein, a buried current
beneath the speechifying, to burst through
finally with tempestuous force, or else
subside to grumblings, rustlings, mutterings,
he thinks of wind and water.
And when he writes of water and of wind,
oceans and streams and boulders, tossing leaves,
he sees and hears the human face and voice
of strife. On earth, in heaven,
tenor and vehicle, vehicle and tenor,
the meeting is uneasy.

Anxiety Attack

omnia pervolitat late loca
— Aeneid VIII.24

The skittering flittering rapidity
I recognize, the turning everywhere,
bat in the bedroom caroming off the curtains
or pale moth blundering around a light.
How exactly do thoughts move at night?
Virgil depicts it as perpetual motion,
the body stretched out, weary —
I have to sleep, I have to rest,
tomorrow is the battle —
while sparkles spangles spackles of anxiety
spatter and splash beyond our will or wish,
like moonlight crazed on water
or slats of sunlight broken up by branches
or errant beams that sweep over the ceiling.
Just so the hero's mind — our mind — careens
up and toward and then again away from
the object of anxiety,
zigzagging even as the body rests.
And what is not an object of anxiety?
Count sheep: safe, pastoral, predictable,
one at a time. Count anything. No good:
a squirrel wheel, a tape loop, not a flock,
the mind is not a quadruped. It spins,
flies, springs, returns, and comes again to rest
a moment, only to zoom off again,
ceaseless motion hooded in our skulls.

Filing System

quaecumque in foliis descripsit carmina virgo
digerit in numerum atque antro seclusa relinquit:
illa manent immota locis neque ab ordine cedunt.
verum eadem, verso tenuis cum cardine ventus
impulit et teneras turbavit ianua frondes,
numquam deinde cavo volitantia prendere saxo
nec revocare situs aut iungere carmina curat:
inconsulti abeunt sedemque odere Sibyllae.
　　　　— Aeneid III. 445-52

In my stone study
I write my poems and arrange the pages
a certain way. But every time the door
opens even a crack,
a draft blows in and scatters all the leaves,
which flutter to the ground, their order gone.
Who's knocking? A delivery? A gift?
Another manuscript to blurb, another
request for a letter of recommendation?
It doesn't matter. The least breeze spells chaos.

The hell with it. Let my new order be
disorder, enigmatic, aleatoric.
It's not as if I ever
numbered my pages. This was not a novel.
Carmina: verses, poems, spells, enchantments,
charms, prophecies. Aha. Each separate leaf
encodes a destiny.
So let them come to me to learn their future
incompletely, which is how we see things;

out of order, which is how we live.
Let them knock at my stone door
and interrupt me. Let them take any one
leaf and make sense of it. I turn my back
on these disordered pages. And then what?

Will there ever be more *carmina*?
I do not know where my own words come from,
or if they are my words.

Stride for Stride

Aeneas maesto defixus lumina vultu
ingreditur linquens antrum, caecosque volutat
eventos animo secum. Cui fidus Achates
it comes at paribus cuius vestigia figit.
multa inter sese vario sermone serebant . . .
— *Aeneid* VI. 155-9

Sad-faced, staring at the ground,
Aeneas, having left the Sibyl's cave,
tosses blind scenarios back and forth.
But not alone. His faithful
companion is right there by his side.
Taking their time, conferring in low voices,
they pace together, worry matching worry,
stride matching stride.

Fidus Achates: my Latin teacher taught us
to snicker at the epithet as too
predictable. But that's not how I see it
now. The companion, the fidelity,
the sharing of a burden
too heavy to be carried all alone —
far from predictable. Precious and rare.
Your younger brother is your dear Achates.
Worry matching worry, stride for stride,
you pace and talk together a long time.

The Mothers on the Wall

stant pavidae in muris matres oculisque sequuntur
pulveream nubem et fulgentes aere catervas
— *Aeneid* VIII. 590-1

The fearful mothers standing on the wall,
the cloud of dust they follow with their eyes:
millennia pass, and nothing's changed at all
of our self-inflicted miseries.
Young men stamping; clouds of dust their feet
stir up; the gleaming weapons and the heat —
the women, poised and fearful, gazing down
as the squadron marches out of town,
keep following its progress even when
nothing is left to see of all the men,
horses, lances, banners. Only air
trembles and registers that they were there:
dust devils, horse manure blown on the wind,
a fume of sweat are all that's left behind.
Nothing more; the life has passed. But still,
stricken, the mothers stare down from the wall.

A Female Cry

volvitur ad muros caligine turbidus atra
pulvis, et a speculis pecussae pectora matres
femineum clamorem ad caeli sidera tollunt
     — Aeneid XI. 876-8

Not just any clamor, any cry,
but a female cry,
the voice of women from the life of women,
plural, collective, the many and the one.
A cloud of black dust rolls toward the ramparts
where they are planted, witnesses and mourners,
whose cry reaches up to the stars.
Does that cry equally reach down
to the parched playing field, the battleground
where dust devils first formed and gained momentum?
Hard to imagine. Even if it does,
no one down there is listening.
And when the women's cry
stretches to touch the stars,
then do the stars respond?
Or, aiming somewhat lower than the stars,
do the gods listen to that female cry?
And if they do hear it, do they answer?

The Cause

Lavinia virgo,
causa mali tani, oculos deiecta decoros . . .
— *Aeneid* XI. 476-7

The cause of all the woe (Lavinia? Really?)
casts down her shining eyes — a modesty
that may be saying "Do not look at me,
do not blame me. This war was not my doing.
Something has been set in motion here.
I am a manikin standing on the wall.
Even as I look down, I am a pretext,
a flapping flag a crowd can recognize
and so salute. I am a hoisted pennant,
a brightly colored banner on a pole,
thrust up from yeasty chaos like a flower
that sprouts from marsh soil,
its brilliant petals nourished by the muck;
an icon of the war but not the cause,
not the instigator,
not the reason, if there is a reason,
that draws the women and the children
up onto this rampart to offer gifts
to the goddess and to show me off —
heroine, princess, daughter, villain, victim.
Please may I step down now?"

Hope: The Secret

spes sibi quisque
— Aeneid XI. 309

Hope: hugged to its possessor like a secret
wish you mustn't tell.
If you spill the secret,
your wish will not be granted.
It may not be granted anyway.

Subway or street — look at the morning faces.
Memories of nightmares, dreams,
lovemaking, arguments — all these
are coded, illegible, locked in the eyes,
barricaded behind the lips.

Hope is more closely guarded than all these,
more deeply buried. Hope: to each his own.
Something we have in common, hope is shared,
yet also profoundly private.
We're all afraid of something:

hope is the twin of fear.
Whatever it is we hope for, we desire.
That we desire it means we don't possess it.
That we desire it means we're incomplete.
And none of this — fear, desire, incompleteness —

is easy to display or to acknowledge.
All are a little shameful.
Each of us goes around
hugging the tender secret
of our separate hope.

The Source of Thoughts

this fire in our hearts

Nisus ait: 'Dine hunc ardorem mentibus addunt,
Euryale, an sua cuique deus fit dira cupido?'
— *Aeneid* IX. 184-5

Tell me, do the gods implant
this ardor in our minds — is it an add-on?
Or flip it: maybe we ourselves
attribute to the gods
our hearts' dear direst wishes?
Or take it one step further: could it be
that what we wish becomes a god to us?
Do things work outside in or inside out?
Top down or bottom up?

The passage I have fixed on — did it fly
from some high dusty shelf, some mottled page
straight into my mind
or did I rather, happening to revisit
the second half of the *Aeneid*
for the first time in more than fifty years
pluck the waiting words
fresh from the page like immemorial fruit?
Or (on the third hand) did my own
fears and wishes conjure up the passage?
Oh my beloved, where do thoughts come from?

In Vain

umeris nequiquam fortibus aptat
— *Aeneid* IX. 364

Onto his strong shoulders
Euryalus fits in vain the plundered swordbelt.
This may mean that he fits it onto shoulders
which are strong in vain
because, shoulders and all, the man,
however strong and young, is doomed to die.
There is another possibility:
although "in vain" is strategically located
in between "strong" and "shoulders" —
umeris nequiquam fortibus —
"in vain" refers not to the body part
but the idea of arming in the first place.
In vain he buckles the seat belt over his lap.
The difference may be subtle, but it's there.
Either way, the adverb slices through
an action both habitual and hopeful
cruelly as a stiletto.

Lucretius was another Roman poet
who liked the somber tolling of *nequiquam.*
But unlike Virgil, Lucretius wields the word
more as a conjunction, a connection
summing up some pattern of behavior
only to dismiss it all as hopeless:
nequiquam quoniam
followed by a gloomy disquisition:
our human purposes, if we only knew,

will come to nothing.

               Sarah Ruden translates
the thought "in vain" by adjectiving it:
Euryalus, she writes, fitted the sword belt
"on his strong, doomed shoulders."
But Virgil's sense of doom extends its shadow
well beyond two blades of youthful bone.
Doom darkens the entire enterprise.
Strength is in vain, heroic ardor, weapons.
The fault is not with bodies or with armor.
Dira cupido, Euryalus called
his lust for this sortie, nocturnal, risky.
He was right.

Carrying the Future

attolens humero famamque et fata nepotum
— *Aeneid* VIII. 731

Do we bear our futures on our backs?
No, our pasts, would be my first response.
We're Marley's ghosts bound up in clanking chains
that drag behind us. When Aeneas leaves
Troy in ruins, hoisting his old father
onto his shoulders, isn't that the past?
Yet with his other hand
he clasps his little son's as they escape
into their destiny. The loads we carry
tangle up the was with the will be.
Each year our pasts seem heavier to carry.
Palpable weight starts pressing on our necks.

In Italy (Troy, the lost wife behind him)
Aeneas is unable to interpret
the fame and fate of future generations,
yet reading them as images rejoices —
images depicted on a shield
he hoists up to his shoulder
in happy ignorance of wars to come.

Pristine, untarnished, free of rust, dents, blood,
the future is a shield that we inherit,
decorated with the coming exploits
of our descendants. So we test its heft
and pick it up and drag it into battle —

proleptic heirloom, magic talisman,
defense of mortal bodies squeezed between
all that happened and all that will happen.
Bowed down by double weight, we stumble on.

Rejoicing in the Image

rerum ignarus imagine gaudet
— *Aeneid* VIII. 730

Ignorant of things, rejoicing in the image,
not knowing the situation, delighting in the picture,
illiterate in history, conditions,
events, facts, the republic, and the world,
fluent in pixels, swiftly flipping channels,
we suck up spectacle as entertainment.
Icons glint and wink and tell the story.
        Reality
is one enormous screen at which we gaze
smitten, lovers fixated
on the seductive cosmos
locked in one another's glassy eyes.

Ignorance

non ignara mali miseris succurere disco
— *Aeneid* I. 630

hanc ego nunc ignaram huius quodcumque pericli est
— *Aeneid* IX. 288

rerum ignarus imagine gaudet
— *Aeneid* VIII. 730

haud ignarus eram, quantum nova gloria in armis
et praedulce decus primo certamine posset
— *Aeneid* XI. 155-6

That drumbeat of *ignarus:* ignorance?
Call it unequal knowledge, our veiled vision.
Sometimes unveiled — not ignorant of evil,
Dido knows to help her fellow survivors.
Jagged asymmetry of what is known:
cosmic irony, remote and cruel
as we blunder around in the half-light,
but also on occasion warm and human,
when ignorance spells shelter and protection
or at least good intentions.
Euryalus wants to protect his mother
by keeping her in ignorance of his
foray into danger. King Evander
wants at the same time to protect his son
Pallas from battle and to let the youth
glory in his first combat — he remembers
that joy and that excitement. And Aeneas's

ignorance also functions as protection:
not knowing what the future has in store,
he can take pleasure in seeing it depicted —
the flip side of his *lacrimae rerum* moment,
when precisely knowledge of the outcome
touches his heart and wrings tears from his eyes,
the bittersweet delight of recognition,
seeing the story he already knows.

Ignorance:
always asymmetry of what is known;
perception's wavering beam
in the vast field of darkness,
vulnerable as we see it tremble.
And always pity. Dido's
pity for the Trojan refugees.
Euryalus's pity for his mother.
Evander's pity for his slaughtered son
and for his own indulgent memory
of young men's fervor when they first taste battle.
The poet's pity for the battered hero
drinking in a future
he will not live to see.
The poet's pity for all those,
which is to say all of us,
doing their best, doing our best in the half-light.
Pity for our lopped perceptions. Pity
for how we try to cope with partial vision.
Pity for the way we parse the story.
The owl of history, wrote Hegel, flies
only as darkness thickens — in which twilight
(he didn't write, but I do)
the poet and the artist do their work.

Grief and Solace

solacia luctus exigua ingentis
— *Aeneid* XI. 62-3

The zany disproportion
between grief and consolation
indicates a deeper disconnect:
the yawning gap between inside and outside.
But which is which?
If grief is an interior emotion,
then consolation is exterior.
Yet grief as a sensation feels tremendous,
much more massive
than what covers or fails to cover it.
Too great a sorrow for this slender solace?
Too frail a comfort for this heap of woe?
We try to match them up, to make them fit,
hoping either to stretch the consolation
so it can reach to bandage the whole hurt,
poultice the whole raw and oozing sore,
or else hoping to whittle down the wound
to fit the meager balm of consolation.

Sometimes the consolation and the grief
match perfectly, as when a mother comforts
a child who has fallen down and scraped her knee.
As she scoops up the child, her loving gesture
dovetails with the hurt. The hurt's a small one;
so is the consolation.
The child turns to the mother, who is there.
But in the absence of the mother, who
to turn to?

After being pulled out of the classroom
and told his mother has died,
David Copperfield, left alone
in the headmaster's sitting room,
studies his own face
in the mirror over the mantelpiece.
The child alone with shock and grief
looks at his sorrow; it looks back at him.
Perhaps his swollen eyes and tear-stained cheeks
offer some consolation.

Aeneas sends a thousand picked attendants
to the funeral of Pallas, the slain prince.
Their presence may not help old King Evander,
Pallas's stricken father; but their absence
might have wounded him a little more.
We do what we can; it is never enough,
our gesture meant to soothe
raw lamentation gaping like a wound.
For such great loss, small comfort.
Solacia luctus exigua ingentis —
even the word order demonstrates
the checkered nature of experience.
The dark corrects the light.
The kindness cancels out the violation.
Inadequacy battles the immense.

The Herbalist

ille, ut depositi proferret fata parentis,
scire potestates herbarum usumque medendi
maluit et mutas agitare inglorius artis.
— *Aeneid* XII. 395-7

Whom we love we want to help by teaching
what we know, our specialties, our arts,
and make them into copies of ourselves.
But the beloved has their own agenda.
Arrows and augury and music — none
of these could help to cure a dying father.
Iapyx preferred to study
the healing properties of herbs,
to practice in obscurity this skill,
also obscure, unrecognized, and shy,
the practice and practitioner both humble,
close to the ground, the way herbs tend to grow,
unacknowledged till a fragrant tincture
helps draw the arrow from Aeneas' leg,
stops the pain and bleeding, restores the strength.

Iapyx chose to learn the art of herbs,
or maybe it chose him, for he was mortal.
He didn't care about Apollo's gifts;
he cared about his failing father. True,
the herb that heals Aeneas' wound is plucked
by Venus. Venus is Aeneas's mother.
But Doctor Iapyx' story, as he struggles
to find a perfect herb to fit the case —
this is the poignant piece. Iapyx is old.

Teacher and student; lover and beloved;
father and son; mother and son;
wound and cure. Herbs can ease the pain,
but they cannot give eternal life,
a gift the gods themselves
should not, cannot easily bestow.

Looking On

gaudentque tuentes
Dardanidae, veterumque agnoscunt ora parentum.
— *Aeneid* V. 575-6

More than pleasure, more than entertainment,
the intensity of looking on.
The youth compete — it's field day — and their parents,
watching, recognize familiar features
of those who came before. Three generations,
all of them voyagers through space and time,
old city to new city
(these games an interlude en route, a respite):
those in midlife whose sons ride, wrestle, shoot;
the sons themselves, whom the spectators cheer;
and finally, these being funeral games
in honor of Anchises, Aeneas' father,
 the elders, some of whom will not reach Italy —
those forebears' faces, those familiar features.

Each time my father used to take me to the playground,
we would see other fathers, other mothers
intently watching as their little children
(I was little too) climbed, slid, and swung,
proud; rejoicing in the recognition
of familiar features; worrying —
all three. If any eyes could ever reach
out like arms and grab a little body
as it fell, these parents' eyes would do it.
"See?" my father would say.
"He's saying to his little girl 'Be careful.'

The language doesn't matter. All the fathers
and mothers here are saying the same thing."
He pointed out the pattern from which we
were not exempt. When I slid down the slide
or when my father pushed me on the swing,
he said "Be careful" like the other fathers;
but not before he taught me he and I
were part of something bigger than our dyad;
were figures in a pattern
that stretched in both directions, back and forth,
Ascanius to Aeneas to Anchises,
all of us voyagers in space and time,
the little girl, the father
old enough to be her grandfather,
Riverside Park, Troy, Rome.

The Long View

tantum aevi longinqua valet mutare vetustas
— *Aeneid* III.415

Unfathomable, geologic time's
power to change is too vast to take in
even if we could perch above the earth
and spy the mountains shrug, the seas go dry.

The first warm Sunday afternoon in April
we're sitting on the grass in Central Park.
Here changes are too minuscule to see.
Latticed in tender green,

life's variegated throbbings look as still
as scattered nappers felled by the noon sun.
But half an hour is enough to show
this soporific lull is an illusion.

The angle of light shifts.
Picnickers stand up and fold their blankets.
Unfathomable mutability:
Camilla will be three months old tomorrow.

Their Own Particular Day

Stat sua cuique dies
    — Aeneid X. 466

Achilles, just before he kills Lykaon,
reminds the weeping suppliant that he,
even he, the goddess-born, the greatest hero,
some morning or some afternoon or evening
will die. In the *Aeneid* as in the *Iliad*,
death often hangs around the battlefield,
but can appear at any time of day —
day not as in the angle of the sun,
the earliness or lateness of the hour,
but as a measure of our mortal limit,
a boundary, a wall
you reach and cannot cross.

Each person has their own particular day.
We know what that means; know
what will follow. Know and do not know.
We remember and then we forget
and need reminding and forget again.
Each person has their own particular day,
but shrouded in contingency. And fate?
Is that day allotted when you're born?
Not necessarily; rather you move toward it
steadily. It stands still and you approach it,
this border you will reach in time and space,
yours and no one else's,
invisible until you're face to face.

And You, Catiline

hinc procul addit
Tartareas etiam sedes, alta ostia Ditis,
et scelerum poenas, et te, Catilina, minaci
pendentem scopulo Furiarumque ora trementem.
— Aeneid VIII. 666-9

Where do we go when we die?
How much space will we take up
and in which region of the afterlife?
How will we be remembered, if we are?

I had you in the wrong post-mortem zip code.
That deep green valley where Anchises ponders
the names and deeds of his descendants — this
is not your neighborhood. The mythic realm
where an enormous vulture feeds
eternally on Tityos's liver —
this is not your destination either.
You aren't in the underworld at all,
but elsewhere, hard to find,
a helpless figure dangling from a cliff,
trembling before the faces of the Furies.
And to add insult to damnation,
you're nothing but a detail on a shield —
one cameo of many from the future.
Once menacing and now diminutive,
perpetually suspended, you are neither
alive nor dead. Your crime is never mentioned.
Aeneas cannot know it; Virgil's audience
do not need to be told.

And what of us?
I am stopped by that apostrophe —
te, Catilina —
the poet turns and speaks to you
and down the centuries I think I hear pity.

Where do we go when we die?
How can a name, fame, personality
score a space on the elaborate shield
divinely hammered out for the hero's use?
Aeneas, its recipient, admires
his splendid gift; but wielding it in war,
he will forget the figures it depicts.

In the *Iliad*, the action stops,
allowing us an interlude to study
Achilles' shield, another godly gift.
Achilles' shield encompasses the cosmos.
The hero nevertheless, consumed with grief
for his dear dead Patroklos,
barely notices the splendid object
which the poet lovingly describes.

Where do we go when we die?
Aeneas. Achilles. Patroklos.
And you, Catiline.

No Way Out

proxima deinde tenent maesti loca, quem sibi letum
insontes peperere manu lucemque perosi
proiecere animas. Quam vellant aethere in alto
nunc et pauperiem et duros perferre labores!
fas obstat, tristisque palus inamabilis unda
aligat et novies Styx interfusa coercet.
                    — *Aeneid* VI. 434-9

Fate is the obstacle.
Fate stands in their way —
fate and the gloomy marsh that hems them in,
fate and the ninefold coils of the river Styx.
The geography of the underworld of suicides is
        overdetermined —
first fate, then the unfriendly marsh, and then
the river, in that order.
Or else not in that order.
What about biology?
Or what about the language of a vow —
a vow, however mistaken, however regrettable,
not to be taken back?
What about time's arrow,
which shoots one way and cannot be recalled?
Space, motivation, second thoughts, the blank
wall of what has been done and can't be undone:
death sentence, life sentence
cramped and infinite at once.
Obstat. The obstacle. The absolute.

One can allegorize the marsh as depression,
the Slough of Despond.
The river Styx with its ninefold loops
could be the whorls of disastrous DNA.
Marsh as mood, river as inheritance:
dire signifiers all too easy to label.

Once the impulse hardens to decision,
once the decision is made,
it cannot be revoked.
Even so, having leaped
off the George Washington Bridge or the Golden Gate Bridge,
and having hurtled toward the water glinting down below,
the jumpers say that even as they fell
they felt regret.
The jumpers who survived to report on their experience.
Some of those who survived.

Better to endure poverty and hardship
but breathe the air, the birthright
and privilege of the living,
than fling away their souls, forego the light.
Achilles — not a suicide but resentfully dead —
says to Odysseus "I'd rather be a wretched
hired man and alive
than lord it over all the bloodless dead."
The underworld is overrated.

Once the impulse hardens to decision,
once the decision is made,
it cannot be revoked.
The powers of gravity, of weight and water,

the miserable sucking swamp, the river
and one-way time (or call it fate) conspire
to block the suicide's return to air.
The act trumps the regret.
The resolution trumps the might-have-been.

Iron Chambers

ferreique Eumenidum thalami . . .
— Aeneid VI. 280

The iron chambers of the Furies — why
iron? Because those chambers are forever.
Discord, her snakes of hair
bound up with bloody ribbons;
the false dreams sheltering under a great oak's leaves;
the sleepless eyes of Rumor
winking underneath her every feather:
all these phenomena, however fearful,
seem organic, perishable, bio-
degradable in the capacious fullness
of earthly and unearthly time. But iron?
Iron doesn't readily wear out,
doesn't change, and neither do the Furies.
They're laws, they're principles, like gravity.
Their modus operandi
admits of no deception. They go to work
and then retire to their iron bedrooms
and lie down on their army cots and sleep.
Their ditsy neighbor in Hell's dormitory,
Discord: those bloody ribbons that she wears
in her snaky hair — she's borrowed them
from the wardrobes in those iron rooms.

Placid and Harmless

amplexus placide tumulum lapsusque per aras . . .
libavit dapes rursusque innoxius imo
successit tumulo . . .
       — *Aeneid* V. 86; 92-3

The enormous snake
that pours its length around the funeral mound and then the altar
turns out to be calm,
not intent on doing any harm.
Having sampled all the appetizers,
tranquilly sipped from bowls of milk and wine,
nibbled, if snakes can nibble, at the sweetmeats,
it switches course and eases its way back
into Anchises' barrow, hefty, harmless,
and (we're not told but can imagine) silent.

What to make of this
calm, this harmlessness?
Gratitude; relief; above all, awe.
Powerful, appearing out of nowhere,
menace withheld, its purpose never clear
but its demeanor placid,
the serpent is a prodigy, an omen.
Uncanny manifestation;
equally uncanny vanishing.
It comes, it does no harm, it flows away.

My son's friends James and Emily
used to own, perhaps still own, a snake,
a pet snake (white? Is that possible?)

they named Elizabeth.
When they introduced me to Elizabeth,
"She's very kind," one of them said.
Kind?
Placid, harmless might be better words.
The blue and golden rainbow-spangled snake
that manifests so gently
after a funeral
is neither kind nor unkind.
At most, this snake is more benign than neutral.
A little more benign.

We see a snake and we think *hiss* and *strike*.
Nor is there any shortage
of terrifying snakes in the *Aeneid*.
But this big one, retreating
into the hallowed earth from which it slid,
is more a shining memory fished from sleep,
is more an apparition from a dream.

Iron Sleep

olli dura quies et ferreus urget
somnus, in aeternam conduntur lumina noctem.
— *Aeneid* XII. 309-10

Harsh repose is weighing down the lids.
An iron sleep takes over and escorts
lights into endless darkness.
Iron: cold and hard. Lights: living eyes.
No sooner does an outside force press down
than the dynamic shifts into a vision
less weighty but still terminally somber:
twin sparkles fading into dimness, twinkling,
blinking on and off as fireflies do
or Lesbia's sparrow hopping down that long
path to a blackness that will know no dawn.

Iron sleep; repose and heavy lids;
bright glances shepherded toward lasting gloom:
there is more than one way to see and say
what is never named, nor needs to be.
Not only that one warrior fell in battle.
All of us will succumb to iron sleep.

Special Effects

poenorum qualis in arvis
saucius ille gravi venantum vulnere pectus
tum demum movet arma leo…
— *Aeneid* XII. 4-6

indum sanguineo veluti violaverit ostro
si quis ebur, aut mixta rubent ubi lilia multa
alba rosa, talis virgo dabat ore colores
— *Aeneid* XII. 67-9

The wounded lion shaking out his mane,
snapping the spear point planted in his side —
Turnus rages like that.
Ivory from India, stained purple-red,
or roses and lilies mixing up their tints
chase their colors over the wet cheeks
of Lavinia listening to her mother
and blushing with compunction, shame, or fear,
helpless, exhibited high on the wall.

Ivory, roses, lion,
borrowed from the world beyond the war
and set into the poem,
jewels on a grimy ground, remind us
there is a world elsewhere. And then the battle
resumes, and the horizon shrinks again,
but not before we've glimpsed the Punic plain,
the wounded lion shaking out his mane,
the Indian ivory. We have taken a tour
and come back to the climax of the battle

all in the compass of a single sentence.
In writing, said Neil Gaiman, unlike movies,
the special effects budget is unlimited.

Who is our tour guide? Who is it who speaks?
Who compares an agitated face
to ivory stained with purple,
lilies and roses blending white and red?
We suck the pictures in,
savor them, and move briskly
back to a battlefield
more vivid now, more readily imagined
without considering who has imported
from the farthest reaches of the empire
lion and ivory and set them before us
before nudging us away again.

Eagle and Serpent

utque volans alte raptum cum fulva draconem
fert Aquila implicuitque pedes atque unguibus haesit,
saucius at serpens sinuosa volumina versat
arrectisque horret squamis et sibilat ore
arduus insurgens . . .
               — *Aeneid* XI. 751-5

The interwoven, implicated, meshed
struggle between the eagle and the serpent:
scales talons hissing mouth and whipping wings
inseparably grappling. Do we
root for the eagle? Or that wounded snake,
bristling, if snakes can bristle, rearing up
its scales erect like gooseflesh? This is not
Pope's wounded snake that drags mimetically
its slow length along in retarded meter.
This figure is of battle to the death,
two panting warriors dueling for control.
Which of the pair can strike the fatal blow?
Precarious confrontation in midair:
snatched from the ground, the snake
perilously dangles, while the eagle,
dragged down by its opponent's heavy coils,
like a struggling swimmer treading water
beats its wings for dear life.

The figure is of battle,
but it feels more like politics: the snake
insurgens, a guerrilla,
perhaps less powerful (an underdog?)

but desperate, dangerous, no easy prey.
The eagle's feet are tangled in its coils,
the talons clutch the sinewy wounded body.
The battle is suspended,
hangs in the balance and is left to dangle
even as our eyes move down the page.

Painted Full of Tongues

fama, malum qua non aliud velocius ullum:
mobilitate viget virisque adquirit eundo,
parva metu primo, mox sese attollit in auras
ingrediturque solo et caput inter nubile condit . . . .
monstrum horrendum, ingens, cui tot sunt corpore plumae,
tot vigiles oculi subter (mirabile dictu),
tot linguae, totidem ora sonant, tot subrigit auris.
Nocte volat caeli medio terraeque per umbram
stridens, nec dulci declinat lumina somno;
luce sedet custos aut summi culmine tecti
turribus aut altis, et magnas territat urbes,
tam ficti pravique tenax quam nuntia veri.
Haec tum multiplici populos sermone replebat
gaudens, et pariter facta atque infecta canebat . . .
　　　　　— *Aeneid* IV. 174-90

Fast-moving Rumor, growing as he goes,
timid and small at first, gains strength in motion
until he bumps his head against the clouds.
Swiftest of evils, flitting through the night,
Rumor never shuts his countless eyes.
He has as many eyes, tongues, ears as feathers;
flies, watches, talks, and listens all at once,
incessantly. He's everywhere. He's growing.
Broadcasting dappled bulletins all day
from a high tower, filling people's minds
with bubbling streams of babble
where true and false inextricably blend,
panicking whole cities, full of glee,
gigantic, disembodied, all hot air,

he goes about his tasks: unmaking meaning
and sowing terror. He can't be controlled
or ignored, he doesn't stop, relentless.
Nor do his crowds of lackeys ever sleep.
Pariter facta atque infecta — reportage
in a steady stream. He never tires.
We are tired. What should we believe?
Fear, confusion, anger — all exhausting.
Crouching in his tower, he pouts and glowers,
angry and happy, happy to be angry,
and keeps on putting forth a froth of words
true and false mixed — but falsehood trumps the truth.
Virgil's *Fama* is female. Not this time.

Weaponized

furor arma ministrat
— *Aeneid* I. 150

Anything can function as a weapon.
A frying pan, a plate,
a vase of flowers hurled against a wall.
A fork. A bat. A ball.
A memory, a dream, a single word
misheard or overheard;
an outstretched hand whose calm trajectory
clenches; a glance that morphs to evil eye.

How can a casual,
all but unconscious gesture suddenly
waver, transform as in a funhouse mirror
from humdrum into hate?
What baleful intervention
poisons an intention?
A nameless impulse skids across the mind
and weapons are at hand.

Poetry Out Loud

foliis tenatum ne carmina manda,
ne turbata volent rapidis ludibria ventis,
ipsa canas oro.
　　　　　— *Aeneid* VI. 74-6

Don't leave your songs to chance,
to fickle winds that play
with what you sing or say.
If your lines are tossed
and scrambled out of order,
their meaning will be lost.
You can read the future,
so tell us what you see.
This is spoken word:
to be understood,
your verses must be heard.
Do not risk the absurd
of aleatoric shuffle;
randomness would muffle
your authority.
Speaking here as your
student, interpreter,
and executor,
I am begging, Sybil,
say your lines yourself.
It saves a world of trouble.
Chant the words to me.
Papers on a shelf
will yellow, blow away.
Capricious breezes play

havoc with intention;
the fitful winds of time
reshuffle meter, rhyme,
rhetoric, invention.
Say your songs to me.
Your verses must be heard.
This is spoken word.

Above and Below

quae gratia currum
armorumque fuit vivis, quae cura nitentis
pascere equis, eadem sequitur tellure repostos.
— *Aeneid* VI. 653-5

devenere locos laetos at amoena virecta
fortunatorum nemorum sedesque beatas.
largior hic campos aether et lumine vestit
purpureo, solemque suum, sua sidera norunt.
— *Aeneid* VI. 638-41

The gratification of possessing chariots and armor,
the pleasure of maintaining splendid horses —
these joys outlast our transfer to the grave.
Therefore (do I have this right?) to read
or write a poem, or to cook, play tennis,
make love, hold a grandchild, bask in the sun,
lose oneself gazing at a work of art —
the satisfaction all these give the living
accompanies us even after we
move underground. This being so, it follows
that chariots, horses, tennis courts, classrooms, books,
eggs, honey, gleaming vegetables and fruits —
all these descend as well
in tandem with the mortals who enjoyed them
while we walked the surface of the earth.

Perhaps it is only facsimiles of such earthly pleasures,
replicas, that follow us below.
But follow to a realm without a sun?

How can groomed horses glisten
if there is no light?
How can you read a poem
or memorize a baby's
features in the dark?
Is the reward of virtue an eternity
of recreation in a skyless world?

No worries; for this has been given thought.
A certain quarter of the underworld
has been provided with a sun and stars
and air — a different air, a larger air,
and special shimmering light,
as if a private sky
stretched like an eternal awning
over the virtuous and fortunate.

Meanwhile on the surface of the earth
horses are sacrificed at funerals.
Weapons, jewels, food, and clothing are laid out
for the departed to enjoy en route
or after they reach their destination.
Utensils are provided.
No comfort is omitted. Nonetheless,
pleasures transported to the afterlife,
as poems do, lose something in translation.

The Author

Rachel Hadas is the author of numerous collections of poetry and essays, and is also a translator, whose verse renderings of Euripides' two Iphigenia plays were published in the spring of 2018 by Northwestern University Press. Some of Rachel Hadas's other recent books are *Questions in the Vestibule*, poems (Northwestern, 2016); *Talking to the Dead*, essays (Spuyten Duyvil, 2015); and *Strange Relation*, memoir (Paul Dry Books, 2011). The recipient of many awards, including a Guggenheim Fellowship in Poetry and the O.B. Hardison Award from the Folger Shakespeare Library, Hadas is Board of Governors Professor of English at Rutgers University-Newark, where she has taught for many years.